ON THE MOON
YOU SHARPEN STONE

Maiche Lev

ON THE MOON
YOU SHARPEN STONE

by Maiche Lev
All Rights Reserved
Copyright © 2019 HDW Publications

This book may not be reproduced, transmitted, or stored in whole or in part by any means, including graphic, electronic, or mechanical without the express written consent of the publisher except in the case of brief quotations embodied in critical articles and reviews.

Cover and book design by David Bricker

ISBN: 9780997575767

http://www.maichelev.com

I dedicate this book to an artist, a sound engineer, a guitar player, and a gentle Rastafarian named Rara Kuyu. Long time at "Tap Tap" on 5th Street. Ra, you were always there with an open ear, some easy wisdom, and of course, a pretty ol' gal on your arm. I say, "A semitic angel was raised when you came," and Jerusalem — Jerusalem can come to you, sir.

*"Jah live, children, yeah.
Jah-Jah live."*

Contents

Possible Alternate Titles for this Book 1
A Furthür Dedication 3
On My Gravestone 5
You Can Close Your Eyes (Sleep Now, Love) 7
Ancient Chinese Secret.. 11
Alfa Romeo Ad: Sunday, August 33rd, 7:00 am . 13
If the World Had a Taste 15
And Learning and Learning................................ 17
Today's Blues 21
Drummer Wanted: Ringo, DJ, Watts 25
Rained Out at the Fair.. 29
Sprout... 33
Lirot Im Shem (for Haadit)................................. 35
You're a Bear 37
Jenn Glass 39
Dear Mother... 41
Well, Hello Dolly.. 43
Delusional... 45
Halloween 2018.. 47
Piece of Work 49
Things Ya Gotta Unlearn.................................... 53
Cream... 55
Want a Cookie? 57
Times, Days 59

On and On (Stephen Bishop) 63
To the Astrophysicist Who Thinks He Knows
   Something 65
Preference 67
I've Heard That Before 69
Drowning Despair 71
The Day that Comes.. 73
Last Word with… 75
Robert Johnson 79
And From There She Peered Over
   (A Greyhound Dream) 81
Cliché 83
The Arts 85
You Will (Reggae) 93
Searing 95
Whitney Houston Died 97
Janet Jackson 101
All in the Shadows 103
You Were Here 105
Beneath the Surface 111
Little Criminals 113
All There Is 115
Jimmy's Place Hiring 117
Pretty Good Band at the Time 119
Sinead 121
Mine Eyes 123

On the Moon You Sharpen Stone — iii

Sorrow Bound... 125

Worst Kind 129

The Night of a Thousand Pornos 131

Fowl in Delaware 133

VMA 135

Hippyhood 137

Failure 139

Second Bridge 141

Evil, Pure 143

Tiberius 145

Once in a While 149

Heroin 151

Black Bart.. 153

The Flecktones 155

Sunshine Orchid '87 157

John Prine in a Second(with D. Bricker) 159

A Capella 163

Shame Shame Shame.. 165

Bapp! 167

In Another Man's Arms.. 169

What Happened?... 173

If I Needed You.. 175

I'm 177

Last Stop Before the End of the World............. 183

Shelved 185

The River Bridge (January, 2017)....................... 187

Friday Morning, 7:00	189
Pleasantville	191
Who Are You, Anyway?	193
Are You Jesus?	195
He Taught Me Everything	197
The Precipice Howling	201
Go See the Gypsy	203
Remember Duane Allman	209
A Couple of Dreams Spliced	211
Ron	213
Last Piece of Black Licorice	215
Oh, These Gays	217
1012 Baar Street: 3:30AM	221
150 Years Ago (with Dave Bricker)	223
Emerald Green	227
Gone	229
The End	233
Tiers	235
Acknowledgments	239

ON THE MOON
YOU SHARPEN STONE

Possible Alternate Titles for this Book

Darth Vader's Middle Name was "Eartha"

Bombin' the Fish Pond

Happy as a Rat in a Cheese Factory

Last Piece o' Black Licorice

LaToya's Berry

Anchorsville Bridge

The Prayer for the Masochist Hung on a Grand Sadist's Bedpost

Ilk County Jug-band Tablature Series III

On the Moon You Sharpen Stone — 3

A Furthür Dedication

Somewhere out there
Is Brad Delp
Boston's great ethereal singer…
Is he warm and dry?
And for that matter
Is he wearing the crown, still?
Its precious stones
Domains of radiance
FM…

Day is night in New York City
Smoke, like water, runs inside
Steel idle trees to pity
Every living thing that's died

Gonna hitch a ride…

On My Gravestone

What do I want on my gravestone?
    Two words:

        Where's Yoda?

You Can Close Your Eyes
(Sleep Now, Love)

Sleep's a companion
Is it not like a lover?
So sweetly I sleep here alone
It beckons
Sleep
You're tired
You go to it
You lie down
Relinquishment
Engagement
Rest falls over you with a feeling so pleasant
Pretty soon … nobody's home

A vagary of ecstasy…
And like would another
Sleep covers
The day is gone

Beneath you
With you
Around you
One
Sleep's trace

The stars
Predictable but changing
Yearning
Speaking
Running
Falling
Dreaming meanings…

From out of the darkness comes a light
Ecstasy
Fantasy
Misery
Prophecy
Profundity

> *Well the sun is surely sinking down*
> *But the moon is slowly rising*
> *So this old world must still be spinning 'round*
> *And I still love you*[1]

And oh…
Last night was I bothered…
A child will sometimes awake in a fright
I didn't get to sleep at all last night!
No…

---

[1] Taylor, James, "You Can Close Your Eyes"

I didn't
Bed bugs leave a mark when they bite
I should catch some Discovery
Or read a book

Goodnight

Ancient Chinese Secret

A boy is not a man
A man is not a king
A king is not an angel
Angels are not free

Alfa Romeo Ad:
Sunday, August 33rd, 7:00 am

A roaring engine with daddy at the wheel
A roaring engine on challenging, twisting
 pavement
Little Johnny in back
With his banana peel
Adoring wife
Cut to aerial shot

Giulia
Go, daddy
Subaru love
Ram tough
Like a rock
The ultimate driving machine
Infiniti

Continental minimalist cowboy Frank Lloyd
 Wright ferry boat ride
Uncomfortable silence
Lipton plunge over-the-top cocaine
 angst complexion
Heifer lamb pony nirvana Zen-man

And…
Hiawatha's sweet horsey "30–Love" grip
   on the wheel
Of this year's model chartreuse sedan
You've come a long way, baby
Lookin' so good!
What people won't do for power…
And *that* little of it

IF THE WORLD HAD A TASTE

If the world had a taste
It'd be … beets
If the world had a taste
It'd be …rust…
Or blood…
Or woman

If the world had a taste
It'd be the air before the rain
Or root beer…
Or molasses…
Or … liver and onions
God *loves* liver and onions
(It's a bit of an acquired taste, really)

If the world had a taste
It'd be Nutrogena T-gel Shampoo

If the world had a taste
It would be pita in the old city
And of course, hummus
If the world had a taste
It'd be fennel

Yes … black licorice
(It's all yours, Vicky)

But most of all
If the world had a taste
It would be the first thirsty, warm water
Out of a summer garden hose

AND LEARNING AND LEARNING

And the airplane glue melted the big foam wings
And the hornets met the young boy throwing rocks
And his stubbed toe bled off the pedal in the street
Breaking up a dog fight will get you bit
Digging in a sand pile can suffocate a child
   if it caves in
Two parents talking at the beach leaves a
   child drowned
Absolute beginners don't belong in recording
   studios
Sometimes no one comes to a surprise party
Quoting movies can lead to embarrassment
Sneakiness is always traced
What's powerful is also dangerous
Preying on another's reputation doesn't feel right
And it's hurtful
Exaggeration is a form of snobbery
Forcing notes leads to an ugly strain
Even though you've got the serum, don't drink
   the poison
One who has waged intolerance always claims to
   have your best interests in mind
Look not for answers where no answers can
   be found

Do the things that only you know best
(Of course)
If you need somebody you can trust,
 trust yourself[2]
You can't beat the house
You can't change the will
Spiritual warfare is a thing of slaves, too
Gambling for support is a "big boy" concept
With toddlers, check windows and drive carefully
Drunks are mean and junkies lie
The sound of a child
Dragging an acoustic guitar around the house by
 a broken string…
Such is life

Some peppers are like flame
You wonder if your flesh is actually *burning*
Women aren't impossible
They deal with a much greater complexity
Cynicism is hiding something it buried long ago
The universe turns on both love and hate
What is labeled "abominable" should be studied
Subjecting yourself to horror movies…
Why?
And pornography?

---

[2] "Trust Yourself," Bob Dylan

(Well ... it's free and it's someplace to go...)
Some are actively hacking their present into a future of wickedness
Some are surrounded by angels ... as vacant as the wind
Astrophysicists say space is cold
Okay ... All souls suffer some shame
Hell is only a single scream that cleanses
Chase beauty; make *what?*
Vice is where the devil finds his darlings[3]
Love is not an evil thing
Nor is it entirely Hallmark

Don't put your horse in front of your cart
Politics is corrupt ... Everybody knows that
John McEnroe was such a minsky-pinsk
Björn Borg wouldn't step back on the court to give him the honor

I like to think I can talk to and get along with anyone
Long enough to share a few honest words...
And *git!*
I'm not slow

---

[3] Spoken by Penelope Cruz in *Murder on the Orient Express, November, 2017*

I just never figured out VHS programming
To record Soap on Thursday Night
And that's good enough for now
(Or was it Tuesday night?)

TODAY'S BLUES

One in every one-hundred children
Gonna have some form of deficient attention
One in every one-hundred children
Gonna have some form of deficient attention
One in a hundred… the number keeps changing
You've heard it mentioned

The act of creation is a sacred deed
It calls for support and protection
The act of creation is a sacred deed
It calls for support and protection
You'll never do something as important again
What have you, dear boy, in terms of momentum
  and direction?

Responsible, law abiding citizens
So busy by day
Deeply dreaming by night
Responsible law-abiding citizens
So busy by day
Deeply dreaming by night
Anything else is so impossible
Could be wrong…
Could be right

What would the ride in the womb be like
 with a diva?
What would the ride in the womb be like
 with a love?
What would the ride in the womb be like
 with a diva?
What would the ride in the womb be like
 with a love?
A concert pianist?
A long-distance runner?
A swimmer?
A lawyer?
Or just someone to love

They say the ground starts t' shakin
That the river catch fire
That the debate is over and done
They say the ground starts t' shakin
That the river catch fire
That the debate is over and done
The price of doin' business
Those pesky, no good regulations

If you're not living well, travel wide
If you're not living well, travel wide

On the Moon You Sharpen Stone — 23

The bass and the snare
To the toms with the cymbals that ride

One in every one-hundred children
Gonna have some form of deficient attention
One in every one-hundred children
Gonna have some form of deficient attention
One in a hundred… the number keeps changing
You've heard it mentioned

DRUMMER WANTED:
RINGO, DJ, CHARLIE WATTS

Thomas Earl Petty wasn't a beggar
Though his heart was true
He wrote with excise
In six lines
Or more if he wanted to
"I changed the lock on my front door…"

Not that it's anyone's business…
But I had a dream about Stan Lynch a few
　nights back
Stan was Tom's original drummer in
　the Heartbreakers
In Gainesville in his teens
Stan was a hot kid on the skins
Tom—a few years older—smiled
And picked him up
And wouldn't let him go

Stan and Tom were legendarily adversarial
Bandmates for years
Stan's drums were deep and huge
Tom's voice
Thin and soaring

In this dream Stan's presence was apparent
He had on a three-quarter-sleeve baseball shirt
The streets and sidewalks around were torn up
Like an earthquake had struck
And destroyed the neighborhood

Nighttime
The sky descended
And a row of chalky teeth appeared
In an almost burgundy colored celestial dome
Lights were on
Sort of humming in the 70s Daytona Beach
  T-shirt stores
Fluorescent lights on a main drag
Cars, sedans, nothing sleek or memorable
I was in the street
'Cause the sidewalks, again, were impasse

I didn't wake up feeling I'd learned anything
But I sure remember Stan Lynch's mug…
And the whole scene…
That overhead view of human dental form
Was a little creepy, y'know…
But telling

On the Moon You Sharpen Stone — 27

Tom made us sing
He made us move, fly, rage, and yeah
If you were with him,
He made you cry some, too
And he knew what he was talking about

A badass, an outlaw, a sweetheart, a Wilbury
Tom said that Stan Lynch suffered a type of inferiority complex in the beginning
Rock and roll has its share of virtuosic monsters
Stan was in awe of Ringo
So, Charlie Watts…
And Stan had to come into his own like everybody else
He and Tom played thousands of songs in as many hundreds of shows
Rock stars
Heroes
Brotherhood
Friction
Strife
It's all in the same bag with a wet cat thrown in it
Whatever it was…

The band changed
And the great Steve Ferrone got the gig
We danced with him too, yes we did…

A year later
October third
Nothing on the newsstand with Tom Petty
 lookin' out
Nothin'

Tom lives in our hearts
And Stan Lynch's drums were as bold as y' could
 ask for
Always kept me
That band did
Always…

Tom Petty and the Heartbreakers

RAINED OUT AT THE FAIR

Oh, the carnival on a rainy day
A rainy day at the fair
Slippery floors on the merry-go-round
The clowns can't be found anywhere
The bumper cars are all abandoned; they won't go
And the tea cups are all scattered so
Gates are closed
Rides are down
Parking lot's empty 'cept for some guards
    standin' 'round
Caged are the lions and tigers
Roped off is the petting zoo
You can hear the lambs and goats *bleeeaat*
And the prize-winning cows in the mud,
    they *mooooo*
Nobody's serving ice cream cones
The cotton candy machine doesn't drone
The trashcans are stuffed with husked corn
The Himalayas still
Silenced its siren's spinning horn
The only lights you see are the lights on the bridge
    between midways
And the flickering string over the wide,
    puddled walkways

The sword swallower and the knife thrower both
    stayed home
The fat lady and the strong man and little
    Tiny Tim
They must be playing cards
Or in their trailers all alone
No stuffed animals to win
No holdin' hands with your girlfriend
No rockstar mirrors
Or Coca-Cola bottles all distorted and weird
No water pistols to shoot
Oh, look at those silly girls tryin' to stay dry in the
    photo booth
No one's singin' in the music tent
Maybe we can go to the grill and get some leftover
    chicken on a stick
This drizzlin' rain; it just won't quit
Heck of a way for your Saturday to be spent
No raffle
No auction
No bingo
Tarp's been thrown over the 'Whack-A-Mole'
No onions 'n' peppers 'n' sausage in the air
Remember that time y' got so sick on the Zipper?
Can't even throw dimes in the Coca-Cola mugs

The toothless vendor just sits there and shrugs
Not much to do at the carnival on a rainy day
Sorry kids
No tickets bein' sold at the fair
We should have checked before we came
Yeah, we should have checked before we came all
 the way the hell out here

Sprout

The seed planted found purchase
The roots spread
The fruit budded
And the yield turned from green to red

From predator and pestilence … protected
Pruned by hands ex-perienced
By precipitation fed
Quenched

Once ripe the limb bended
And bounty
The harvest
Providence

Picked
Peeled
Pitted
Peared
Pickled
Processed
Packaged
Propagation…

Produce
Provided
Posted
Pleased
People

Profit

A pittance

The seed planted found purchase

On the Moon You Sharpen Stone — 35

***L*IROT *I*M *S*HEM (FOR HAADIT)**

The boy: the sea
The girl: the earth
The boy: the spirit
The girl: the soul
The boy: the sun
The girl: the moon
The boy: the knife
The girl: the bread

You're a Bear

Don't make love to your woman
On your first night in the woods
Or she'll turn into a bear
Really…
Ten o'clock the next day
Growlin'

"What are we doin' so miserable out here
So buggy and hot
With no running water…?"
Water

Stanley!
Blackberries!

Jenn Glass

I once crossed paths with a woman named Jennifer
Who insisted on being called "Jenn"
She told me there were times in her life
When the sound of breaking glass was her
   only consolation

She told me she was a child of adoption
And that she and her mother were often at each
   other's throats
"Come on," she said
And we went outside
She holding an orange juice glass
She'd snagged off of her messy dresser

We stood for a moment in the late afternoon
In the middle of the street
A quiet enough, very affluent North Bay Road
On Miami Beach

So, this broad-shouldered, dirty blond *wings*
   the glass
Like a boy
Like she means it
(Like she's practiced)

Lobbing it thirty-five feet high
And *that* far forward…
And … *crash!*
I could understand the draw

A couple of years later
She got me high at a Zeppelin tribute show
No … it was Dark Star in Hallandale

I hear she got married and moved to New England
I can just hear them in New Bedford
"That woman from Florida
She'd better sweep up after herself
Or I'll call the police again"

I'm sure she still walks around the house in red underwear with the windows open
I'm sure she still smokes marijuana when she drives
And like a kid with a pirate smile
I'm sure she pockets a glass at every dinner date
    or lunch
Jenn Burns

Dear Mother

What would you say up-front
That you learned about mankind, dear mother?
Your boys and your girls
The way they held themselves
How much they were the same
How much they differed
The dissimilarities between their fathers
Their voices
Their expression
Their laughter
Their stride
Their posture
Their gait

This one's a climber
This one's a dreamer
This little girl has to have the most cake
This one is after God's own heart
This one…
Our Henry Lee
He never stopped blowin' once he picked up a harp

Dear Mother
You are rich in daughters and sons

Did you think it would be this way when you were young?

"No … God, who could?"

WELL, HELLO DOLLY

A high thanks to Dolly Berthelot
My second editor-at-arms
With you, Dolly
I've laughed with a kid of the Louisiana spirit
Been challenged by a fine writer
An American girl at heart
I knew I was in good hands right away…
But especially at the end of our sessions
When you'd quietly say
"Now you … *Get out*"

Love ya, Doll
And my first draft's for you any time

—Maiche, Pensacola 2018

DELUSIONAL

Yes, I am delusional
But only insomuch that I always — or sometimes
Steer my mind
By trying to make sense of my world
Through the letters and numbers in
   abbreviated poetry
Spelled out in the license plates ahead of me
   in traffic
But only on watermelon-raspberry-colored
   automobiles
(And all Ferraris)

Halloween 2018

She come knock on my door this Halloween
In nothin' but a raincoat
And a red clown nose
Josephine Mookiyonim…

I fell to my knees
My forehead to the hardwood
She told me to "Get up!"

When she put her hand on my shoulder
And asked me to get up again
I hugged her waist
Refusing to let go
Refusing to stand

We collapsed together
There…
Just inside the doorway
I kissed her face
And kissed her face

Then we *lost* it…
Two little kids

A Casper and a pirate
Witnessed our embrace
And we decided…
That's to be our ritual every Halloween

Trick or treat, my sweet love?

Piece of Work

I'm a piece of work
But I'll shine when I'm through
I'm a piece of work
But I'll shine when I'm through
What d' you think, Johnny…?
In a hundred years
Could we shake this voodoo?

He ain't another white boy singin' black
He ain't some punk … on the attack
He's hardcore as the next guy
Kind as a priest
As I'm tied and bound
So shall I be released

I'm a piece of work
But I'll shine when I'm through
I'm a piece of work
But I'll shine when I'm through
Can't go on a tour of forty countries or more
Got plenty right here to do

He ain't another white boy singin' black
He ain't some punk … on the attack

Hardcore as the next guy
Kind as a priest
As I've been tied and bound
So shall I be released

Oh, I'm a piece of work
But I'll shine when I'm through
I'm a piece of work
But I'll shine when I'm through
All kinds of answers for all kinds of questions
I got my walkin' shoes

He ain't another white boy singin' black
He ain't some punk … on the attack
He's hardcore as the next guy
Kind as a priest
As I've been tied and bound
So shall I be released

I'm a piece of work
But I'll shine when I'm through
I'm a piece of work
But I'll shine when I'm through
Well I guess it is…
What you've put up with is as much or more than anyone would…

Or should

Still, he ain't another white boy singin' black
He ain't some punk ... on the attack
He's hardcore as the next guy
Kind as a priest
As I've been tied and bound
So shall I be released

—Eurail, Amserdam, '89

THINGS YA GOTTA UNLEARN

I do not know the necessity
Of perpetually balancing
Metaphysical astrology
And spatial philosophy

The homegrown
Where you come from…
There's your meditation
There's your greater identification
And within it your vision…
Your knowhow
Your rhythms
Be free
Take from there!

So much for *The Portable Nietzsche*
Something for nothing is everybody's game…

Lourdes is gone from us now
Settling in somewhere

Namaste

CREAM

"And that's not how it had to be"
 Eric Clapton said of his recently deceased friend,
   Jimi Hendrix
 Eric said he felt a kind of anger at Jimi
 Over having left them there without Him

WANT A COOKIE?

When good people follow shallow reasoning
Into poor decision-making
And then into more poor decision-making
So disestablished…
A problematic existence
Led by a crowded personality
Is what remains

And it doesn't end until the mistakenness
Leads to a jail cell
Or a broken mind
Destroyed lives

Want a cookie?

TIMES, DAYS

There were times
There were days
When…
You'd like me to have understood something I
   wasn't getting

There were times
There were days
When…
You thought it was acceptable to leave a fraught
   soul fretting

There were times
There were days
When…
All was to me a crime

Times
And days
When…
Turning away from love
Might have made you sooner mine

There were times
There were days
When…
I knew you were a servant
Who would be a servant no more

Times
And days
When I knew
Your beauty was something hidden
And I knew it was not just the other side of myself
   I was living for

There were times
There were days
When…
I knew you were monopolizing

There were days
There were times
When…
I knew I was doin' the same damned thing

There were days
There were times
When…

By dreams summoned
By dreams condemned

There were times
There were days
When…
I was no more than the sand
Beneath the point of a pendulum

There were days
There were times
When…
It was all new to me
Like some mystery
It could even have been like a myth[4]

There were days
There were times
When…
I could feel the weight
Of the life of one
Who never took somebody close to share it with

---

4   Bob Dylan, "I Don't Believe You."

On and On (Stephen Bishop)

Poor old Jimmy
Sits alone in the moonlight
Saw his woman kiss another man
So he takes a ladder
Steals the stars from the sky
Puts on Sinatra and starts to cry

To the Astrophysicist Who Thinks He Knows Something

Equinox
Celestial Tangelis
Aplomb acclaim buttress
Aplomb acclaim buttress rivále
Meniscus
Reflux
Luminere
Equinox
Borealis
One-thousand dances
Celestial Tangelis

And that thing Noah Klein used to say
    about effervescence

"Say, can I have some of your purple berries?"
"Yes, I've been eating them for six or seven weeks now
 Haven't got sick once"

Preference

Preference?!
My preference went out with the Yugo, man!

And if you insult me with one other word…

I've Heard That Before

Be "something-something" like a man
Do "something-something" like a man…

I made love to a woman
After quite, quite some time
Tears flowed from my eyes down her temples
Trembling
We just held on
Breathing
Together
Almost … preternatural
Wheezing and whining
And we laughed some, too

I told her everything…
She in her fifties
A late child of holocaust survivors
Allyssa…
We were so attuned

On the Moon You Sharpen Stone

DROWNING DESPAIR

I wanted you underneath me
When I made re-entry
Drowning despair
But I guess nothin' from nothin' leaves nothin'

I haven't kept company with women
Re-entry
That was the reason
I haven't kept company with anyone…
And this you knew, Mehrav

There's always some raw emotion
That's obvious only when it's exposed
Lady, I don't mind dyin'

No one's going to win a blue ribbon for
   blessed virgin
No one's a saint who hasn't sinned
It's just that I've crossed this desert
To find you on the chaise lounge
Kissin' on him

There's a line in a song about comin' to a river
And somebody pays the other's fare

The man *with* something
It's in his shadow
Thieves *thick* you'll find there

Everything the evil monkey can do
The evil monkey has done to me
I'm dancing all around
Almost like a child

I don't do so well without some
   distraction anymore
To get real stoned and listen to *Desire*
You were the one none of 'em wanted to ride
You must be a Leo ... or a Scorpio
I'm standing in a house
Its cinders cashed

In some way I know I'm part responsible for
   this insanity
Despair's effect on one's own physicality
I chose to suffer
And have since succumbed
And then this…
Jesus…
Exponentially

The Day that Comes

If I'm alive on the day you die
What will I feel?
What will I know?

She was everything other women are not
She dealt no pretention
Her natural beauty breathtakingly warm
I'll know as I always have
That I walked out on a love of completeness
That I've blown it in my life in more ways than one
That with her I should have known better

We loved each other
Respected and admired each other
She gave me a perfect boy
Ten fingers
Ten toes
And she named him

Her powers were vast
Born of humility
Not conniving or vindictive
She kept nothing up her sleeve
Nothwithstanding the occasional hairball

She was bravehearted with hash pipe and…
She was kind
She was … Big Bird
And I never apologized for breaking it up
For breaking her heart
Oh God…
I do, Jill
I apologize…
To myself first

We were great
I was a mess
Still am

Last Word with…

I gave you that sweet song
I remember…
Four or five years before I wrote it
I kept seeing all the life around your house
And how it was still there and enduring
Upstairs and down
Your beautiful family
And all of our rock and roll friends about
And I suggested a title three or four times

And … nothing…

So…
After hanging out with y'all
I found myself back in Jacksonville
In bed
And I got up
I knew I could write it myself
While you guys were still on my mind
And so I did
And that night I dreamt of a woman
Who had arms like the infinity symbol…
(How strange to remember so pointedly)

And what have you given me back, dude?
Attitude the worse
A disgruntled, practically non-verbal,
 nonspecific rebuttal
Like I'd stolen something of yours
Gotten too close yet again

Fuck that!

It was more than just a good bit of writing to me
Am I to apologize for doing something for you
That you were unable to do for yourself?
Namely, delivering up a heart and mind
Your own
Sorry…?
The double-minded
The split-tongued
The well practiced
The bit-timed
Hearts as hard as leather
Hollywood motherfuckers in brown socks
Oh…Look out!
You must still have some things to "work on"
 after all
Imagine that

On the Moon You Sharpen Stone — 77

Well I guess Billy Bragg can roll over on his cot
In the back room of the cantina "Lady with a Fan"
Somewhere in the Mojave
We spoke of "unconditional friendship"
Unconditional friendship is a non-sequitur
Without reciprocating interest
¡Responsa…!

We haven't been able to be as brothers —
   or even friends
Since my drastic actions some thirty years ago
That something you are able to speak about
   with others
But have never had the heart to mention or
   discuss with me

All beautiful words and ideas tied together
Unremarked upon
By a syllable of gratitude or thanks

ROBERT JOHNSON

On Robert Johnson selling his soul to the Devil to
   play that way
Please...
Such simple theological platitudes are for
   Hollywood dweebs
And bored nostalgia buffs

Look...
A black man in the south had no ride
His compass pointed to the next shanty party
Not even a juke joint
So he walked with his guitar
Shoulder-strapped its case
A change of clothes and some worn-out shoes

Think of his jumpin' style
Walkin' blues
Long elegant fingers
A clear Mississippi morning
Countless crossroads...
Wakin' up cold in the rain again
"Babe, I'm booked and I got to go"
That came after lots and lots of hard miles

And lest we forget…
The white man calling you "nigger" left and right
"Whatcha got in that case, boy?"

I can listen to Robert Johnson for hours
Where the rest of those blues daddies
Are like the next generation's diesels
Robert Johnson walked and walked with
   his six-string
And don't you forget it

AND FROM THERE SHE PEERED OVER (A GREYHOUND DREAM)

A Tom's of Maine toothpaste tube gooping black
    squares floating upward from a watered-down
    footspace 'neath a bucket seat with a transparent
    container top floating skimmed
A voice spoke the words: "She married someone
    who likewise doesn't give a shit about anything"
Then, the voice said, "Go tonight while there's
    interest." — a reference, I hoped, to an east coast
    bicycle trip to be taken on a Cannondale waiting
    at home
There she stood, one of the boys, looking over to
    me from where she stood, hunchbacked

Whoever you carried the white palm frond for
The tundra's fauna was overhead, not underfoot

That transparent container top 'neath a bucket seat
Was floating on tears
A lot of 'em
So I guess I should 've known
What I'd been told more than once
It'll only make you sad
And how it has

And now
In accordance with my reputation
I'll call Prince Georgie for some righteous cocaine
Must be some way to beat this gloom
Sing a song
Play guitar
Make it snappy!

Cutie pie
Someone's died
Don't throw me a party

He pats you on the back every time you make
   a speech
Kisses you how y' like to be kissed

The sun's coming up
And you really don't approach people
Who are sitting alone on the beach

Cliché

It's cliché
"You were always too good for this world"
Until…
One you can't help but covet is fed to it
And she turns around
Back into the flame

And your gift of fine sandals
None others would do…

THE ARTS

People love the arts
Paintings come alive
Magical moments
You stand there
And all of a sudden
It's as electric as any screen…
Alive!

People love the arts
Something that talks
Something that sings
Something that lurks and stalks
Dances
A play commences
The Arts
A happening!
Pushed every button of my soul
I sat in my seat
Losing control

People love the arts
Mikhail Baryshnikov had hang-time
No matter who you were

Regardless of age
He took your breath away
Sold out for months
They stood in line
The Alvin Ailey Ballet company
The poster alone
Says you're in for a ride of another kind

The Arts
There's lots of ways to make a guitar sound
Can sound like the wind
Can sound like a train
Like lightning striking
A teardrop falling
A punch landing
A woman walking
A world ending
Shredding
Blue eyes crying in the rain
Death
Or a baby's breath
Harmonics

A guitar
Six strings
Scalloped wood

Silver frets
"Gonna leave … this broke down palace"
Garcia
Segovia
All them delta women say
"Hey, that's handsome Dickie Betts!"

The Arts
The Shakespeare Festival
Renaissance
"Madam … I have this dance."
There stands an old-world amphitheatre
Y' need a jacket
Y' need a ticket
Y' need to be on time at the turnstile gate
Red roses for the opera singers bow
You touched my heart, Maria Pagés, and how!

Accolades
Conflict
Honor
Pride
Nature
Love
Death
Poison

Murder

Shame

Tyranny

Mercy

Infamy

Betrayal

More tragedy!

Mezzo soprano

Colora

Contralto

Carreras

Domingo

Pavoratti Luciano

All three!

The Arts

1994

Miami Beach

A traveling company

Grey Poupon

Pommery

Baguette

Pirogues

Brie

Don't forget the connoli!

Backdrops

Costumes

Actors
Stagehands
Groupies
Security

A caravan
Horse-drawn
Tidings
Lodgings
Players
Playbill
Musicians
Special effects
Pyrotechnics
(That's what they had in 1726)
Conductors
Gypsies
And who might you be?

The Arts…
Home-slice
You remember…
Kids making up plays in the living room
Big sister

"And then … well…"
"And then you can…"

"Benjamin, you stand here and say…"
"Ok, ready?"
"No, wait!"
"Ok, we're ready; turn out the lights!"
"Oh, no; the camera wasn't on; start again."
"Daaaaad!"
"Okay…"
"Our summer vacation by the Gustafson's!"
"Take two…"

If I'd 've gone to college
I'd 've probably pursued at least a minor in
   art history
And I'd 've enjoyed it
It would've been the next best thing to being
   Bruce Springsteen
And I'd have married young
She'd 've been a like-minded dreamer
We'd always be half-broke and frugal
We'd be involved in the community
Babies: one, two, three
We'd trip on Matisse, secretly
We'd know what was coming to the Guggenheim
And in St. Pete, the new Dali Museum
(You haven't been?)
We'd have an unbelievably incredible time

On the Moon You Sharpen Stone — 91

Even if the Hallucinogenic Toreador lost some of
  its ... breadth
It seemed
In its new place
To be somewhat confined

And she and I wouldn't suffer
What a lot of other couples suffer nowadays
Our interests long-combined
Almost like children
And we'd laugh
And love the arts like people do
Giggling in a room at an Air-BNB in Prague
For a week
Seven days
We'll be under a spell
And in front of the Louvre
We'll decide for ourselves
Whether I.M. Pei's glass pyramid should be
  left standing
Or felled

And we'd love the colors
The brushstrokes
The canvas
The easel on which this painter painted

"Honey…
 His nose must itch behind the glass
 And his throat probably tickles"

The words
The page
The poet
The author (his room in Florence)

"It's the writer, not the writing"
"No … It's the writing, not the writer"

The songs
The strings
The voice
The singer
Robeson's "Great River"
Basso profundo

The arts
The past
The future
And we'll hold onto each other
Yes…
We'll hold onto each other
What a picture…

You Will (Reggae)

You will…

You will come to your senses

You will…

You will address your weaknesses

You will…

You will stand by your convictions

You will…

You will recognize contradictions

You will…

You will find the note to sing

You will…

You will forgive trespass

You will…

You will transcend intolerance

You will…

You will greet the future on familiar shores

You will…

You will sleep in peace

You will…

You will sustain after having been released

You will…

You will know there is a saving grace

You will…

You will be where you are welcome

You will…
You will reap what you have sown

In the end there is one dance you do alone[5]

And you will find the note to sing
Yes

---

[5] Jackson Browne, "For a Dancer"

Searing

Prince reached 'searing' status
That doesn't happen unless you're a little beastie
Beastie!

Searing…
Never been but a few ever to reach that,
   don't y' know?

I was reunited with a troubled gal
She came back from the store
And announced by the bedroom window
That Prince had died

We walked out
Crossed the bridge off Crespi Boulevard…
And by the courts
The sky was … an impossible five-mile
   straight-blade
Couldn't have been thirty-five-hundred feet up
Look…!
Mia…!
Look!

Whitney Houston Died

Some things are too terrible to be true…
First the beauty of the world
The born star Whitney Houston dies
Then her only progeny
"Lil' Bobbi," they called her
She shuffles off so young and irresponsible
Like she had nothing to live for
Her gracious mother's legacy
She was half of her

Lil' Bobbi angel eyes
The child is gone?
The child is gone
Some things are too terrible to be true

The sadness of it
The loss
Whitney Houston was a born star
A stringbean singing louder in church
A beauty next to you in the school yard
Looking on
Talking low
Laughing out loud
But listening well

She was a credit to her race
A credit to her gender
A credit to humanity
Her skin
Her eyes
Her smile
Her voice!

Whitney Houston

That little Bobbi might have given us five or six children
It wouldn't have been so bad
One might 've sung like Nina Simone
Wrapped in a shawl
Her own priestess
One might 've sung like Marvin
Tall and skinny
A handsome black Jesus
And one would 've…
Some things are too terrible to be true

Somewhere must a light shine
Brighter
Longer

A welcome
Warm and secure for all

The dream of beauty that cannot be taken away
Whitney and Bobbi
Dream on
Dream on

JANET JACKSON

I guess she was seven or eight
To my five or six years
When she came across the screen on Good Times
I swear I remember her actually glowing
Our eyes were cast upon a creature angelic
Just a love

A decade later
Riding high
Having too much fun in the age of MTV
She decided that God's work was to be accented by
  the hand of man
Doctor Drivesaporsche from the Hills

Well, the nurse in the operating room
Balled up the sterile gauze
And down the drainpipe
Went the cartilage
The flesh and blood
Of Janet Jackson's divinely formed countenance
And when the ice-packs were removed…
What?
This sister's moved on?
Where?

No one felt it worse than she
The crimes we commit against ourselves
Against our families
Our heritage
Our God

But even today
I bet Miss Jackson would assume that high, sweet
   voice of hers and say
"I'm very happy with what I've done"

"And who is this fucking Maiche Lev?"

ALL IN THE SHADOWS

The old Floridian's service elevator
Glass-walled
Black doors
Metal rails
And then you…
All in the shadows

Fluorescent zappin'
The overhead lights blinked on then off then on again
There she was as the door opened
All in the shadows

Trapdoors
Gangways
Ambushes
Expensive, pleated, black leather couches
In sunken living rooms
A power-couple's vows
There she was…
With a knife between her teeth
All in the shadows

Money red
Money green
All the refineries in between
That line about love in *Against All Odds*
About the kind of love that won't leave you alone

She starred in *The Thornbirds* with
   Richard Chamberlain
Maegan
Shorn lambs
A priest's temptation
All in the shadows

—Ein Karem, Arbel House

You Were Here

You were here
Standin' right there
Am I not always in the middle of gone?
Didn't you say that you could just shake me
For the way I was?
Withdrawn
Fluorescent lights
Dark glasses on

There were cooking pots on shelves
Double sinks in the kitchen
I read and I slept and I played a mandolin
The river held barges
There, the fog is always lifting

It's laughable really
How many times I've picked up and moved
 next door
To find a place to get it all together
You wanna know what I did today?
Well the first half I spent thinking about
 the present
And the second half was devoted to *forever*
One day ... oh, one day I'll get it together

A superstar's salary
What a landlord earns
A brand-new used car
Twice the light when both ends burn
The Eiffel Tower
The Taj Mahal
The Great Pyramids
The Empire State
Prestige wants not to know
Its unwillingness to reciprocate (Lord!)

One night came an evil shadow
Thrown 'cross the floor in a lightning storm
I walked alone in the rain a good ways
"Coffee please …
The pecan … warm"

Through all these years
The memory of a person
I want to say something but nothing comes
And here come those tears again
Those tears…
Again…
This isn't happening
What have I done…?
What have I fucking done?

I thought of the stars and the planets
How they could lose rotation
I guess you could call this
A dysfunctional situation

Y' don't let a woman like that go by
Cry, baby
Cry, baby
Cry, baby
Cry

The moon has slipped behind the clouds
I'm so lonesome I could die
Cry, baby
Cry, baby
Cry, baby
Cry

Frankenstein's violin
Elvis' blue suede shoes
The first wheel rolling
Some scrolls found up in the hills
A harem whose master's gone bowling

Some live for secrets
Double meanings

Split words
Some find themselves in positions of power
On the ninety-second floor
Well-dressed with poised nerves

You were here
Standin' right there
Am I not always in the middle of gone?
Something about the sisters of mercy
And what its love's inscribed upon

I sure can't say I haven't lost anything
   I might've won
I can't say I'd choose a different path
Than the one from which I've come
For so long
Every day closed just as it had begun (Lord, Lord!)

Your baby brother
The splash in his chest
To hear you once speak my name…
I may have to confess
To the practice of exogenesis

Exogenesis means 'tweedly-dee-dum'
Tweedle-dee-dee

Exogenesis means fiddle-dee-day
Fiddle-dee-dee
Exogenesis means
"Why, aren't you just the pic-a-ninny?"
Exogenesis
That space between things never felt mutually

I wrote all this 'cause it was just more than
　I could do
Yesterday I heard the song "Yesterday"
All my troubles seemed so far away
Now it looks as though they're here to stay
Oh…

More than I could do…
Wish I'd 've put on that apron
And started scrubbin' the skillets in that kitchen
You'll wish your days away
Just end up with a heart more stricken
Yeah, you'll wish your days away
With a mind more messed about
And a year less willin'

You were here
Standin' right there
Am I not always in the middle of gone?

Didn't you say that you could just shake me
For the way I was?
Withdrawn
Jimmy's Place
New Orleonne, '87
Dark glasses on

BENEATH THE SURFACE

Beneath the surface
Some men are conditioned
Or predisposed towards violence

Some men wade in waters
For their blood to become enriched
In its own retentive ebullience

And there's a lot of other kinds o' fellers, too

LITTLE CRIMINALS

I can hyperventilate
And keep rhythm with ya, mama
I can even let my voice out
Show ya what you're doin' to me

But to look right through you…

Someone left their heart in San Francisco
Someone wept on Royal Street
And someone left his soul
On a farm in the Middle East
Some thirty years ago

All There Is

All there is to give been given
Right then and there
She gave
As I have followed, now what have I?
Two steps away from an early grave

All there is to take been taken
Right then and there
She took
As I followed, now what have I?
Here's what was manufactured
Didn't stop once it shook

All there is to dream been dreamt
Right then and there
She slept
As I followed, now what have I?
Lift the shade
We're on our final approach to Zurich

All there is to do, mama, been done
Right then and there
She did
As I followed, what have I?

I know God has mercy on those
Slandered and humiliated

All there is to honor, she donned
Right then and there
Awards
As I followed, now what have I?
Stones and shells
No diamonds
No pearls

All there is to have been had
Right then and there
Was named
As I have followed, now what have I?
Tell me quick, jackass
One more time
Of what have I to be so uproariously ashamed?

All there is to ask for been asked for
Right then and there
She requested
As I followed, now what have I?
Hollywood, USA
Number unlisted

Jimmy's Place Hiring

I guess there'll come a time
When it's my turn to go far-far-away to a
    foreign land
And wrestle with what I see around me
A language I don't speak or understand
Maybe there'll be chieftans
People of reknown and influence
Who'll take a consecrated and undying
    interest in me
And I'll revel in their attention
And be thrilled to death a thousand days
I'll come of age

How d' ya take your eggs, mister?

Pretty Good Band at the Time

Don't let me change my heart
Keep me set apart
From all the plans they do pursue
And I…
I don't mind the pain
Don't mind the drivin' rain
I know I will sustain

'Cause I believe in you[6]

---
6   Bob Dylan, "Slow Train Coming"

Sinead

Sinead
I smell of the earth
I am bored by the weather
I'm in sacking weeks
I'm learning of things very non-royale
I'm misspelling things
Enough of sentences
And Sinead…
Vespidness
Cockney curtsy of the tart
Sinead

MINE EYES

All at once his eyes changed
Like they hardened some
Weighed different
Like my eyes were in little vices
Almost like they were caught

Caught
I felt it walking away from the medicine cabinet
And then walking slow around the apartment
Odd
Optic
And that afternoon on the elevator's
   reflecting walls

All at once my eyes changed some
I'd picked up a few images from a few dreams

—Crespi Boulevard '14

Sorrow Bound

When you're sorrow bound
You know it
When you're sorrow bound
You'll show it

Sleep is a most welcome relief
Wanna curl up into a ball
Hide underneath

Torment is torment
You can't just disappear
I'm sorrow bound…
Can't get outta here

Don't take the world on your shoulders
Don't take yourself too seriously
When your sorrow bound
Rain falls precipitously

When you're sorrow bound
You've dropped the key that turns the lock that
   opens the door
You're feelin' around in the dark

With neither flame nor spark
Solitary is a game changer

When you're sorrow bound
You're on the path reading signs
When you're sorrow bound
The world's so unkind

When you're sorrow bound
Y' need something strong to distract ya
What's gotten into ya?
Shake it off, man!
What's eatin' at ya?"

Sorrow bound
Life and love are everywhere you are not
Water damage
Fire sale
Warped goods
Rot

Sorrow bound
All those proverbs and sayings seem too true
Oh but for the bending of rules
What to do?
What to do?

Where are you?

When you're sorrow bound
You're not so impressed with yourself
The dishes are too much for doin'
The TV belongs to someone else

Sorrow bound
It can't be this way everywhere
What have we done to each other but prove
That life can be so unfair

Sorrow bound
There's a song to be written
A poem to write
From some dreams you wish to be awakened
Deep, deep in the night

When you're sorrow bound…

WORST KIND

The crimes we commit against ourselves…
Worst kind
They're never addressed or redressed
The crimes we commit against ourselves
Are the ghettos we live in, neighbor

The Night of a Thousand Pornos

Look close
And you will see that the form has pockets
Babies in bathwater
Butterflies
Electric sockets

100,000 titles
All pointed the wrong way
What sells gets sold
Then it's put into play, pretty baby!
Good or bad, right or wrong
Forget about it
The devil for one second wouldn't have you doubt it

If you was born with four faces, you'd get rich
You could live on a train
Travel town to town
An endless tour, of which
You'd be talkin' to yourself in a continuous
    dialogue
The mirror in the bathroom would never fog

Silkscreen ecstasy
Polka-dotted sun

One magnificent thrill to the next
Comest upon

Indian bells on ankles
Toe rings on toes
There should always be a woman around
To tell the fool how little he knows

Y' don' fin' Cadillacs inside Cracker Jack boxes
Look close
You will see the form has pockets

Fowl in Delaware

Sometimes now
I think there's either something inordinately wrong with me
Or there are souls I've known who are working things out
In some kind of accusatory intransigence of blind jeopardy
Some of my most lasting and dear connections
Seem poised in some unthinking, incrementally leery aim
Almost like large predatory fowl
Perched on a promenade stilt
Waiting to feed
To swoop down
To tear
Ravenously bobbing
And dumb for its taste

The desert is behind me now
And I wouldn't have you lot stuffed

VMA

You are so fine a human being
You've taken care and respected yourself
Who's that girl?
I sense an electricity
Like a ghost running through your person
Almost apparent
Ever haunting you
Virginia
My God, you've harnessed light!
In New Balance

Great beauty
Long may you run

Hippyhood

Into hippyhood

Where else might I have hoped to have landed?

It's music, loose and unkempt

It's garb, modest

Heightened be its dance

It's tribe, gentle

Everything and anything at any given
 point relative

A confidence

A trust

Y' find God's children in farmers' markets

Patchouli and sweat

But to one day transcend it…

From the quill, feather takes

Failure

A relationship has failed
If the two party's wills only grate
Loaded guns
No way out

God knows…
When all you've learned
Is how to kill one another
You get good at it

And tell me, baby…
Where did we go wrong?

Second Bridge

Got to be an important person to be in here, honey
Got to have done some evil deed
Got to have your own harem when you come in
  the door
Got to play your harp till your lips bleed[7]

---

7 Dylan, Bob, "Sweetheart Like You"

Evil, Pure

"Y' don't think there's pure evil in this world?" asked one mouse to another while nibbling into a dried-up, rock-hard, bear turd underneath four feet of snow blanketing ancient old-growth northern Mongolian tundra on a moonless night in early September?"

"Bear, I'd say. No?"

Tiberius

I always liked the name Tiberius

Aleph

Bet

Vet

Gimel

Dalet

Hey

Vav

Zayin

Chet

Tet

Yud

You don't find that many Ethels or Gertrudes
   any more.

Eins

Zwei

Drei

Vier

Funf

Sechs

Sieben

Acht

Neun

Zehn

Hi

There's nothing wrong with her a hundred dollars
    won't fix

Un

Deux

Trois

Quatre

Cinq

Six

Sept

Huit

Neuf

Dix

Me and my RC

What's good enough for other folks

Ain't good enough for me

One

Two

Three

Four

Five

Six

Seven

On the Moon You Sharpen Stone — 147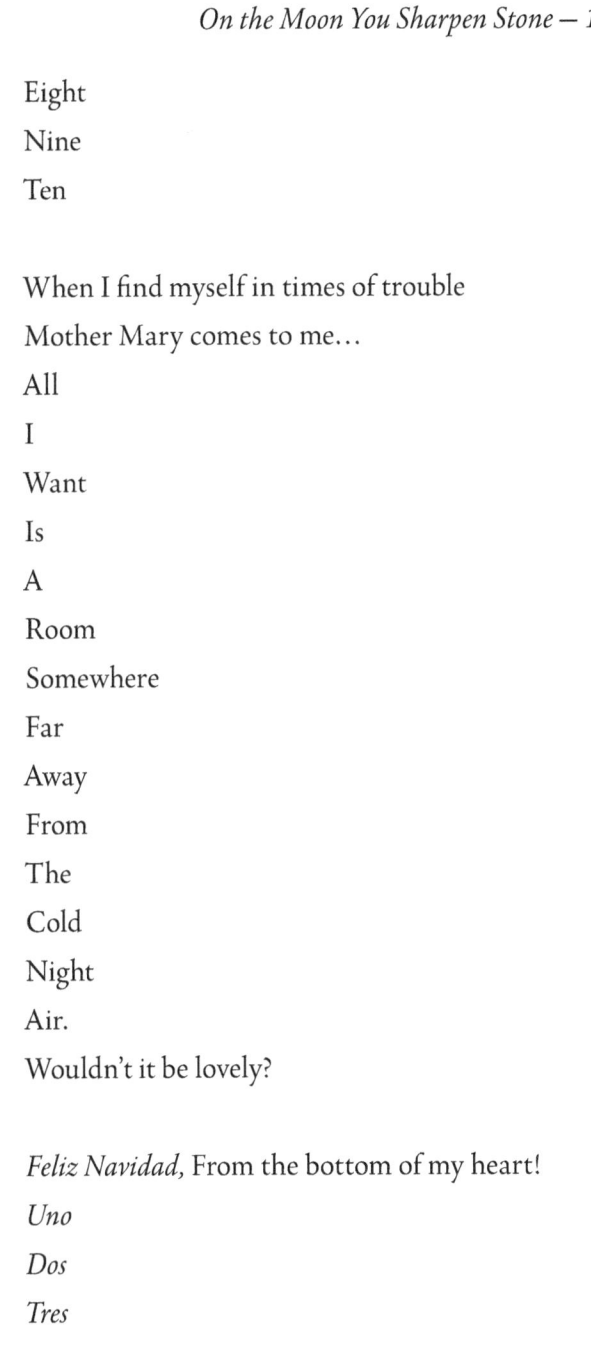

Eight
Nine
Ten

When I find myself in times of trouble
Mother Mary comes to me…
All
I
Want
Is
A
Room
Somewhere
Far
Away
From
The
Cold
Night
Air.
Wouldn't it be lovely?

Feliz Navidad, From the bottom of my heart!
Uno
Dos
Tres

Cuatro
Cinco
Seis
Siete
Ocho
Nueve
Diez

Be all you can be!
Army
Navy
Air Force
Marines

Kumbaya m' Lord
Kumbaya
Kumbaya m' Lord
Kumbaya

Yeah ... I always liked the name Tiberius

Once in a While

Once in a while
It's like I can feel your pain
But I go back to mine
Just the same
Just the same
I go back to mine
Just the same

Once in a while
A crime is a shame
And I go back to mine
Just the same
Just the same
I go back to mine
Just the same

Once in a while
How many days…?
I go back to mine
Just the same
Just the same
I go back to mine
Just the same

Once in a while
I whisper your name
But I go back to mine
Just the same
Just the same
I go back to mine
Just the same

Once in a while
The time that remained
But I go back to mine
Just the same
Just the same
I go back to mine
Just the same

Every once in a while
Love's a losing game
But I go back to mine
Just the same
Just the same
I go back to mine
Just the same

HEROIN

I'm fifty-one years old and I've just discovered
 heroin
I really like snorting the stuff
They call it "dogfood" here in the 'hood
This dirty dust is like ... springtime
Where cocaine is ever clear and ever present
Sexy and ... gone
(Add bourbon and you've got a pussy-driven
 monster pushing buttons at my address)
Yep
I'm fifty-one and I've got ahold of some 'smack'
I'm talking to myself out loud
Never knew I had it in me
"Hey, it's a natural opiate"

I did wake up on the rug in the other room
In a slump
And I don't know how long I nodded off for
My feet on the floor
My chest flat on the kitchen counter...
What?
And in the bath after taking my meds...
Fuck!

It's a gripping high
Turned my stomach so
I had to vomit in the car next to Mike and his girl

I'm fifty-one years old
And I've just discovered heroin
Think this might be a bad idea?
An unforgiving problem?

BLACK BART

A hot shower is a luxury
A warm bath
Heaven

Clean sheets
Almost never
Someone to curl up with
Y' can't remember

Black Bart
A horse
A rifle
Forty acres of land

Black Bart
Your cape
Your belt
Your boot
Your gun
One cried and prayed for you
What is this person to become?

Black Bart
You're a diamond

How does it feel?
You won

Black Bart
Did you trade the moon and stars
For half a bar of gold
On the surface of the sun?

Black Bart
You're a diamond
Black Bart
You won

The Flecktones

It's not about speed
It's a power paw on heavy bass strings, Victor
The banjo comin' out with stuff
Like the invention of Post-its, Béla
Lamar … Future Man …
Is busy texturizing carpets
Flippin' hotcakes in a kitchen
For you … fresh!
Man…!
Béla Fleck and the Flecktones
Go to their show
It'll do y' some good
Psilocybin … mandatory
They don't come to town every day, kids
And Post-its are a kind of magic!

SUNSHINE ORCHID

You know I'm thinkin' sunshine
You know I'm thinkin' light
You know I'm thinkin' that everything, love
That everything, love, is gonna work out all right

I walk in to the kitchen
I walk in to the room
Thinkin' of how it'd be if you were here …
And my soul is an exquisite orchid in bloom

If I could give to you
Just one thing
This world and its wonders
This world and its wonders to you I would bring

—Baka, Jerusalem, '87

John Prine in a Second
(with D. Bricker)

John Prine in a second?
He's the sweet singer you were glad to find
All heart with his own sense of humor…
Minus the swagger

His America is the last gas pump attendant
Walking away from the last filling station
For the last damned time

He's Duval in *Tender Mercies*
A deep sadness
An infectious smile
A whispering voice
A goofy laugh
An inquiring mind…

At his best
The sentimentality of true empathy
Tears in his voice he can't hold back
Only a few of 'em ever get a handle on that

Calls a son-of-a-bitch a "son-of-a-bitch"
Uncompromising…

Yet with a soft side
One who inspires confidence
He's a star
And no folkie in the world has that many girl-
    friends
Must be he's rock 'n' roll after all

His father was no aristocrat
John served in the army
And delivered the mail up north
Probably lives to go down on Bonnie Raitt
(But then they all prob'ly do)
Plays his guitar mostly fingerstyle…
No pick
And he's a licensed cult member deprogrammer if
    you didn't know

John Prine in just a second…

In an Appalachian Greyhound bus station
She sits there waiting
In a family way[8]

Or…

---

8   Cash, Johnny, "Unwed Fathers"

On the Moon You Sharpen Stone — 161

We were standin'
Standin' by peaceful waters...
Standin' by peaceful waters
Oh Woah Wa-ouh Oh woah Wa-ouh"[9]

Yeah
John Prine in just a second
The sweet singer you were glad to find
Bigger than a secret hero
An angel that flies from Montgomery
A poster from an old rodeo

Just give me one thing
That I can hold onto
To believe in this livin's
Just a hard way to go[10]

John's like a kid from a simpler time
Walking out of the house
With a comic book in his back pocket
And an impressive little slingshot he made

John Prine in just a second

---
9   Prine, John, "Lake Marie"
10   Prine, John, "Angel from Montgomery"

A hundred thousand blackbirds
Just flying through the sky
And they seemed to form a teardrop
From a black-haired angel's eye[11]

We all hope you got a hundred-thousand miles
And a hundred thousand more in you, John
How you've touched our hearts
See ya round the tilt-a-whirl

---

11 Prine, John, "Everything is Cool"

A Capella

Aye…
A voice
La vocé
A capella breathes
You're in a dark room
Under a heat lamp
Glowing low

As spoken
As chanted
A melody rises
A chorus haunts
A capella
Its own nuance

You must know your song well
Before you start singing[12]
A capella

---

12 Dylan, Bob. "A Hard Rain's Gonna Fall"

Shame Shame Shame

What to God on you is a shame are the dreams of
  your life.

Bapp!

My glass is half-full
But it's cracked on the side[13]

---
13 Bapp Kennedy

IN ANOTHER MAN'S ARMS

You're gonna die in another man's arms
He'll look into the face
That held all those charms

The love we two never shared
What we couldn't make ours
A love left in limbo
Empty arms…

You're gonna die in another man's arms
Beneath another man's roof
We don't need a roulette wheel
To search for proof

The wonder twins
The strength of skin
The light in your eyes
Post-mortem

An obituary in the paper of some city
It wouldn't have been so bad
If the poor girl had died at home
She never did know what she did to me
I could never make that love my own

Once thrown together
Her and me
Into other lives …
Lived apart
Separately

We never lit a candle in a darkened room
To find each other's faces
Another man's miracle
Another town's oracle
Ten and ten is twenty paces

People in glass houses
Shouldn't throw stones
At the end of his marriage
He wrote, "You're My Home"

It's crazy what we could've had
She went and took up with him…
You look much better with me
Than you could with any of them

Monkey in the middle
Red Rover, Red Rover
Freeze tag
Leapfrog

Dodgeball
You're not anywhere on this earth
Thinkin' 'bout me, tonight
I've got to get that through my skull

We all heard voices for a while
Now the rest is history
Your gonna die in another man's arms
It just occurred to me
And it comes down so hard
And it makes me feel so sorry

How do you end a song like this?
How do you start one?
Son, find someone who'll be to you
A close and true companion
Ain't no use in cryin' your life away
Over any other one

You're gonna die in another man's arms
You stowed yourself away
I'm sure there's a spot in heaven
To park that long, dark blue Bentley

Another man's arms …
He's the one you chose

Over these drained cups
And torn clothes
Spite the face
Pierce the nose

You're gonna die in another man's arms
Congratulations
You came out on top of the heap
A box of faces
What "out of place" is
Straight into darkness
I've seen what's hanging in your gallery

What Happened?

In this life
Has my mind really been your event?
And then…
Is the converse also true?

Your throne would be incomplete
If we just left each other wandering

What *happened?*

On the moon you sharpen stone

IF I NEEDED YOU

If I needed you
Really…
If I was in need
I'd have gone a great distance without
And then a great distance without again
Writing songs no one plays
Writing words no one reads

Once upon a time
A handsome little farmgirl
Thought only of horses
She sat looking at the stars
While a boy across an ocean
Turned up the volume
And tried to sing "Dreamweaver" that way

I'M

I'm paranoid schizophrenic
I'm manic depressive
I'm undiagnosed bipolar
I suffer poor self-image
I've been a user and an addict
I've got an exaggerated sense of self-importance
I'm highly delusional … most of the time!
I'm best friends with compulsive liars and grifters
I hate everyone
I'm an Indian-giver
I'm a stooge to powermongers (and power sluts)
I make promises I don't keep
I never do what I say I'm going to do
I'm snobbish
I think I'm better than you
I'm not overweight; I've been carb-loading
Women are objects to me
I'm a suicide attemptee
I'm a conscientious objector
I'm a great inspiration to the slacker nation
I need forgiveness … but don't know it
I'm the contagion of all things wanting
I collect unemployment and disability fraudulently
And I don't care

I haven't had a job in twenty-five years
I grew up with an addiction to porn …
   or an inordinate enthusiasm for it
I'm short and my feet are too big
No one likes me in the state of Missouri
I was once clocked doing ninety-six miles per hour
While listening to Bob Dylan's *Saved* (Hi, Jill)
I fear death
I abhor patriotism
I'm always right
You could say I've got an attitude
Like Kafka, I hate noise and all forms of hyper-
   popularized drivel
Smooth jazz
Heavy metal
Amy Winehouse acolytes (no)
Vaudeville smells like vomit to me
(Unless they're smokin')
And all that sticky shit they fed us
On major rotation MTV
I don't recycle
Without marijuana, I am a problem
To myself and those around me
I joined the Army and cried my way out
I'm a lousy kisser and I have bad breath
I'm a cheap date

I recognize no hypocrisy in myself
I look like Tommy Lee Jones and Richard Nixon
I pick my nose vigorously
I never wash my hands after I use the bathroom
Gilbert Godfrey is my second cousin
I have body odor
I think I'm special
(Did I say that yet?)
I seek attention using shock value
That makes me obnoxious
I don't beat my dog but I never brush my cat
I suffer a jealousy so strong, my blood type
   has changed
I'm a poster-child for the walking wounded
I only pursue cross-eyed women
I don't read the paper
I talk too fast
I curse
The spirit of revenge runs through my body
Let me tell you what I hate about rap music
I'm computer-illiterate and don't care
I'm fifty and I've never bought a new car
I haven't watched an NFL game since I was eleven
   years old
I don't know what the id, ego, or super-ego are
Small things get the better of me

I have a mind that magnifies the trivial
Without medication, I ruminate
I might be a control freak
It's loving and it's laughter I disdain
I never give others the benefit of the doubt
Or any credit
Time and again, I've given the undeserving
The shirt off my back
I go too deep with others too often
I'm a know-it-all
The rules don't apply to me
I once ran from a burning train
I fell asleep behind the wheel of a sedan
And lost five of my nine lives—maybe more
Do as I say, not as I do
(Of course, the universal truth)
I'm sometimes as deflective as a woman
I'm unconcerned with other people's feelings
I'm short-sighted
I'm full of excuses
I'm a big cover-up
No, bigger than that, Angel!
I think about exercise a whole lot more than I do it
I'm quick to blame
I've been called "gutless" and "a moocher"

And I speak poorly of others
I'm balding
I should be a better drummer than I am

It goes without saying
That sometimes I'm an aggravation to those
 around me
I've made some really poor decisions
I ran out on my wife
After she gave me a perfect baby boy
I've betrayed my own spirituality
I smoke too many cigarettes a day
Sometimes I look in the mirror
And I see a scary dude
I peaked socially and physically when I
 was fourteen
I was in jail for thirty-six hours once
I get hungry and irritable like a child
I'm generally depressed and volatile
I joined the church twenty-five years ago
And didn't even know it
All in all, I still believe I'm redeemable

Solo Cristo salva

LAST STOP BEFORE THE END OF THE WORLD

If you think there is such a thing
As advanced civilizations
With vehicles that move
According to a differently calibrated
 instrumentation
Listen…
No, listen
They took on human form
And they live in the city of New Orleans

Last stop before the end of the world

If you think there's such a thing as holy beings
Ever graceful in their own enlightenment
Dealing with issues from on high
Listen
No, listen
They fell to earth over the city of New Orleans

Last stop before the end of the world

If you think a snarling creature can be dealt with…
Growling

Heaving ribs
Brindle coat
Listen…
No … listen
Quaint…
Deep in the French Quarter
The City of New Orleans

Last stop before the end of the world

Shelved

Love is a prescient being
I've seen her
Made of a white light
She shone
Turning slowly
Slowly turning
Alone
In a courtyard
Moonbeams through limbs
A ghost on rough-cut stone

Prescient
A world with her in it
The shape that time reflects
The face that time reflects
Like I'd never had a thought
Midnight made perfect

And I clung like a hunted child

The River Bridge (January, 2017)

In a painted twilight
By a river bridge
In front of a sunset
Over a low, rolling mountain range
Risen
She tied her gold bikini straps
Effortlessly behind her neck
Looking up and over at me
Hovering somewhere above the river
The sun was blocked by tall eucalyptus trees
The sky turned to a chalky whiteness
Interwoven … tangled
We embraced somewhere in this dream
She in a sleeveless, fuchsia t-shirt
By a rust-colored early '80s Cadillac with those
    spoked wheels
And custom grill
The snake-eyed chap
Wearing a collegiate gray jersey with
    black lettering
He communicated nothing

And I woke up wondering
How and why he was in my dream

I hadn't asked for him
His name: Avivi
Once in an Israeli slum
He told me he'd asked God
Whether or not he should kill me
So, over yoghurt and greens
I looked him in the face, unbelieving
Thinking nothing but…
I know who and what you are…
And I'd like to leave now, please
Why the *fuck* this far down the line
Is this man in my dreams?

A bent-together bottle-top, rusted
Hung suspended in mid-air turning
Where the sun ought to have been
My embrace with the lady
Ended with a noted feeling of emptiness
The driveway: unpaved
Red Georgia clay
Somebody whispered the word "candle"
And I woke up with my usual nothing
Seemed like an event had been waiting to begin
What have you…
Dreams…

Friday Morning, 7:00

Live for love
Live for power
Live to sit back and laugh about it
Staring at the lime
At the bottom of your Whiskey Sour

Did a queen starve a king?
Did she watch her garden weed over
Until the sun rose
Only to set
Right then
Over that mansion in the fields
Where sweetness lost its voice?

Nothing like regret to remind you you're alive[14]

---

14 Cheryl Crow, "The Difficult Time"

Pleasantville

Pleasantville's murky green spire in the sky
Time zones sorta passin' by
A soupy, trapezoidal parallelogram
Floating there
Slippery, foamed, dust clouds
A disturbed surface
This shade of algae … rolling
A swamp above Mars

Oh yes…
Something's always terribly wrong in Pleasantville

A spliced frame of film
A cotton dress on the line in the wind
A nursemaid lovingly thumbing the babe's crown
To see it nicely rounded

Who Are You, Anyway?

It's not your job
It's not anyone's job
But you took it on
Sure showed me…
And the crew

I guess the Dead Sea didn't have enough salt, Haadit

ARE YOU JESUS?

Are you Jesus?
I hope not
I mean … there was an old soul to raise
Once upon a time
But we all run into that blessed combination when we're young

I failed
And dealt with it miserably forever
Life's too fair
Then you writhe

On windy days
We used to buy plastic kites at the store
It really doesn't get any better than that

Are you Jesus?
Once in a while
People say I have his eyes
And once in a while
You hear someone say
"Nothin' good ever come from Nazareth"

He Taught Me Everything
(Pride is Hard)

He taught me everything
We sang
I remember sitting in the front seat
Him singing
Me singing
Windows down
Always windows down
I felt for him a love and joy and awe
Like a son does
For a young, doting father

A sadness in his eyes
Like his sister
My Aunt Debbie
I never asked him why he felt he had to leave
   the states
Maybe it had to do with the woman he wrote so
   much about
Maybe he arrived in a place too upsetting to exist
   in here

My dad
This sweet man

He once told me he knew so much strife
It was debilitating
He told me there were times he knew tears through his week
And that he'd wake sometimes
Mortified
He missed someone terribly
And lost her
But felt he'd earned her love in some way

You don't really get used to dashed hopes
You either get up and change and enrich your life
And live
Or…

He didn't do that
He closed in
Shut in
And refused to lose…
And he turned to stone

I'm going to see him overseas
We haven't spoken a word to one another in seven years
I'm not sure what I'm getting myself into

He was smoking more than two-and-a-half packs
   of Marlboros a day
Last time our paths crossed in Pensacola

The Precipice Howling

And a voice clearly spoke the words:
"You're sad"

Yes...
I am so
I'm full of dread
At the horror of this exclusion

GO SEE THE GYPSY

Go see the gypsy, son
I've already had the wind knocked out of me
Go see the gypsy
I'm all out o' fight
Things got bad on Tuesday
And Wednesday…
Beyond me

Go see the gypsy
And don't bring your whore
Y' need her there the least
Go
Closest thing around here you'll find to a priest
She is

Go see the gypsy
Bring her a new set of cards
Here…
I got a deck last time I's in the Quarter
Bring her a bottle of something good
A few yards of the finest fabric
Bring her a new blade with a handle of elm
And don't mention to that filth that you are my son

She will see you're snared…
That your mind is caught
Tell the gypsy
All came to naught

Go see the gypsy
She'll be in the gloss wagon
Tell her of the dreams y' have over and
   over again
And the vision of the black stallion

And let her do most of the talkin'
Ask about the wedding we saw out in the sticks
Ask her about the troubled one
Who must always be playing tricks
While whispering judgments
Ask about the dust fields in space…
And how the musician stood there
Wearing someone else's face

Go see the gypsy
Tell her your dreams are beyond control, boy
Tell her you were asked to do some things when
   you were younger…

Tell her about the dream where a baby was seen in
   the womb
That water broke over her shoulder
Fully dressed
Breach
Go to her by late afternoon

I…
 The gypsy queen…
Son…
From what you have told me…
I know there is someone you can't let go of
So much so
You refuse to live
You are falling
You are torn
Your dread is as though topped off
You feel the breeze where others do not
You refuse to lose to one who lives to win

Yes, son…
You refuse to lose to one who lives to win

A dark horse in the night means
There are returns you can't receive
'Cause you've saddled all your forces
Dark horses
The black horse is a demon's beast
Its blood can withstand Mercury's fire

Once you were young at heart
Now you're near to a cancelled will, son
Others have used their powers
To exploit your soul
And they have!
And you've let them!
Sometimes you consider what they'd feel
If you relinquished all
Boy, give me your hand again

I'll tell you more, now

The dream of shattered teeth
Is not a thing of sweet talk and wine
They got some beautiful people out there, man
They can be a terror to your mind
And show you how to hold your tongue
They've got "mystery" written all over
  their foreheads

They kill babies in the crib and say, "Only the good
   die young"
They don't believe in mercy
Judgement on them is something you'll never see
They'll exalt you up
Or bring you down main route
Turn you into *anything* they want you to be[15]

If you never knew, son…
The secrets we carry
The secrets we hold
What secrets wield
Secrets kept
Secrets told

Go now!
Your father is still alive
Plague him not with your issues
Whatever it is
He has lived here far too long

How do I know this?
Go enjoy the fire and drink with my people
As I'm sure your father did once
Years ago
'Neath these stars

---

15   Dylan, Bob, "Foot of Pride"

Remember Duane Allman

I think Duane Allman should be studied
At both Julliard School of music in NYC
And simultaneously
In perpetuity
At Berkeley School of music in…
In…
Where's Berkeley?
California, right?

Remember Duane Allman

A Couple of Dreams Spliced

"You sit *here*," he said, pulling up a stool
"He's in his nineteenth year
 What are you doin' here?"

"So what changed your mind?" she asked

What changed his mind…
Was that hot ass and that wild pussy!
"I felt bad for him," he said
"And now he's gone and done somethin' stupid"
Somethin' stupid, m' Lord?

Someone convieniently misread the postcard sent
And for the sake of one dying
Donnie Dufaye and Camile Lovemolle
Proceeded with electric faith tied between
    their teeth
To perform an act of *love* or attempted murder
Self-immolation—hers
And his, the barbecued g-spot grommet
    deep within

This was May 18, 2018
A real gumball rally

Some hours later…
After these super-heated events
She spoke…
"We killed him, didn't we?"

It happened
It works
And white, gold, and green streamers
Upon dismount

And there on the chaise lounge
There on top, she lay
Kissing him
Intoning
"He would never…"

Yeah…
You got me going, baby
You got me gone…
And who could care less…?

And then…
Further into the Old Floridian
Receding with Leon from the sofa
Toward sliding glass doors

On the Moon You Sharpen Stone — 213

Was it something I said?

I sat next to the boxer
Me at his right
And she on his left
Facing Mecca
While the other patrons
Did strange things with the joints of their fingers
Their arms outstretched like zombies
All of them well-dressed in dark blue

To accomplish the first of anything
You have to be able to live with yourself
In your own skin
That is to say…
There has to be something *left* of you

I waited patiently for the Lord
Who inclined and heard my cry
He brought me up out of the pit
Out of the mire and clay[16]

And I will sing … sing a new song
Yes I will sing … sing a new song

---

16 Psalm 40

Ron

McDonald's got plug-ins
And the Egg McMuffin is everyman's
  God-given right

So kroc it up, boys
Free breakfast
Thursdays
Under the arches
5:30–6:30AM

LAST PIECE OF BLACK LICORICE

Ex-wives throw knives
Circus clowns really aren't very nice
Obstetricians love porn
Doctors, sophisticated plumbers
Politicians, recovering stutterers
Lawyers mean well, don't they?
Pilots, alcoholic mannequins
Businessmen know a dog when they see one…

Laborers suffer "roach-coach" envy
Bus drivers' children Spirograph
The Etch-a-sketch is all but taboo
Bank tellers all need coffee enemas before 3:00
Loggers dance reggae in their sleep
Fast food managers, Japanese dignitaries
AM shock jocks
All born cooler-than-thou
NFL coaches, Golem Gargoyles (not Tom Landry)
Fisherman, florists
Self-help gurus, pet psychiatrists (Oh, Matisse)
Singer-songwriters, health food store
   Birkenstock clerks…
Or something far worse

Military men, boys who have to pee
Movie Stars … check the wind with a wet finger
Border guards like a good polka
Farmer's don't play much
And they always give exact change
Teachers, snake charmers
Movie producers, little kings
High school principals stare in disbelief, mostly
CEOs bleed absinthe
Rock stars … all practice hyena mating rituals
Poets
Master thieves
Them all

THESE GAYS THESE DAYS

These days
If you say anything the least bit disapproving
　about homosexuality
You're immediately labelled, "homophobic"
I have a few homosexual friends
And I enjoy their company
No more or less than other people I know
But really, maybe a little more
Gays are nutty, a refreshing change of pace

But the culture of prissy-ness is a lie to me
The dissonance of being constantly argumentative
Is as much a caricature
As any made-up fool
Sorry!

If it's satisfying to them
To call each other, "bitches"
While deciding on cosmetics and costumes for
　the rave
Well … whatever…
Puh …leeze!
The depiction of this supposed feminine persona

Is an insult to women
And blown-out ... and obnoxious
Shut *up!*

What Anderson Cooper does after work
I'm unconcerned about
I like him
He's all heart
And he's smart
And relaxed
And he's fucking Anderson Cooper!

But gay rights may provoke some
    egregious wrongs

A man dressed as a woman in heels
Gets stabbed inside the walls of Jerusalem
On Gay Pride Day
Stupid…
To have marched there
Amongst people of The Book
Try it in Uganda if you're so fucking brave
Or Tehran, sweetheart

Violence visited upon homosexuals…
In the south

Don't be kissy-face in front of 7–11
I don't smooch or twerk my girlfriend in
 public, either
Show some class!
Have some class!

Why does Joe Rebel go for the baseball bat in his
 pickup truck?
Why?
Here's his subconscious raging scenario:

His little nephew sees two men kissing…
Then … on Tuesday
In his second-grade class
Little Billy gives his buddy Adam a kiss
And Adam says, *"Are you gay?*
You're gay!
Homo!
Billy's gay!
Billy's a fag!
He kissed me! He kissed me!"
And now his family has to deal with that shit *forever*
Because kids absorb *everything*
And kids are cruel
And all because of your exhibitionist needs…
Your show of "affection"

If your gay love is real
You should be glad for it
In and of itself
But whatever it is you've found…
Remember
There are more than a few out there
Who will make you a martyr for the cause

If you're a mature person
You don't need to constantly rave
If you're a mature person…
You have no drive to flaunt or will to shock

These days
These gays…
I'm sorry…
But if you say anything the least bit disapproving about homosexuality
You're immediately labelled, "homophobic"

Is this "homophobic?"
Is it?

1012 Baar Street: 3:30AM

There's a nightbird out here every night
I guess he's working things out
Calling out so clear
Noisy as a small pipe-organ

The moon's one day off full
So, I guess his little birdie curly whirly
Went to bed a wreck

150 Years Ago

(with Dave Bricker)

Just 150 years ago
Before Henry Ford kicked it all off
And the Vanderbilts and Standard Oil
Had not yet lit the flame of the industrial age
The great inland waterways
From Miami to Saint Louis
Were teeming with marine life
Still in their primordial, pristine fulness

You could come to Florida
With little more than a knife and some rope
And you could survive
And even thrive

The coconut
The orange blossom
The mango tree and sugar cane
Were abundant and made for the tropics
A sunshine state
An eden

Way back…
A few centuries before…
The "primitives"
The Indian squaw on the Land o' Lakes butter box
Was invited aboard a wooden ship
It's sails tatooed with the flags of the cross
She stepped off
Disease nearly killed the masses

Just 150 years ago…
Now Biscayne Bay is near barren
Seagrass is sparse
Rusted sewage pipes gurgle beneath her
Algae blooms
Coral has long faded
Pollution causeway to causeway

One day, I guess about ten years ago
I saw a lone family of dolphins
Breaching in a sludge of bubbling soap
By the 79th street Bridge near the marina
I got off my bike
Wow … dolphins!
And I saw the six-to-nine-foot mammals spouting and taking air
In this runoff … in this filth

And it hit home
What we're doing to these waters
And how they once were

And another natural encounter…
I was spooning some coffee Häagen-Dazs ice cream
On the sixth-floor balcony of my parents' condo-
 minium one night
And an adolescent five-or-six-foot shark
Swam slowly up near the surface
The full moon was out
And the shark rolled on its side
As if to spy the silver orb
And speak to me
With its white underbelly shining

All the kids in my family are grown now
But we stood on the docks by the canal
And learned to click back the arm of a
 spinning reel
And how to bait a hook with live shrimp

The industrial revolution flourishes all around us
With its boots heavy on our toes

But 150 years ago…

EMERALD GREEN

Dear Jan,
I had an important thought this week
Well, maybe not exactly important, but…
I thought that you
As a mother and recent empty-nester
Should do yourself a little favor
I was thinking you should purchase for yourself
A mid-90s 456 Ferrari M-GTA in emerald green
You can probably pick one up for about sixty-grand
It's a model that doesn't look like a fire-breathing
   dragon on steroids
Not braggadocio…
It's all business
It says … "You have arrived!"
And people don't hardly know it's a Ferrari
Till you start 'er up and she rumbles
Look it up — the 456 M-GTA
Looks good in burgundy, and silver, too
And they made a convertible!
Lest you've forgotten that my birthday's in
   early February

Love you, Jan

                                      —Brother Dave

GONE

An old man with a walker
Struggles to cross a set of train tracks
In the ten-o'clock sun
A bicyclist passes him slowly
Negotiating with himself
To help or not to help

He's doin' alright…
No trains in sight
He'll make it

But he could fall
He's ancient
And if he did fall
The horror!

The cyclist rides past
What the fuck is wrong with me?

Gone

Oh, look
A woman has gotten out of her car to help

But she sees that I didn't help
And thinks everything's okay
And she steps back into her car

Gone

I just let an old man
Probably in his eighties
With a walker
Cross two sets of train tracks…
What the fuck is wrong with me?
Poor form!

And of course, this is more than something that ruins your day
It's another instance in your life
That's a sign of preoccupation
And selfishness
And lack of caring

Am I too wrapped up in my sorry world
To care about others, anymore?
Seems that way
And all that stuff about "doing better next time…"

Okay…
To forgive myself…
Ready?

It's like I'm in mourning
The emotions I'm dealing with
A rape of the mind
And I've written it all in these pages
And there's no laureate's filing cabinet
That I haven't floated in the last ten weeks
And it's gotten to me
And I'm still smoking forty cigarettes a day
And I'm alone
Failed
And "fuck you" doesn't come first
But it's rollin' in like a freight train

Withdrawn
Removed
Just plain depressed
Like I never knew
What it is I suffer has done me…
And done me good
Gone

I'm wrapped up in gone
I'm tangled up in gone
Ha-ha-ha
I'm knocked-out loaded once again

Poor, poor pitiful me
Story of my life
And who'd 've thought words could mean so much
From one so blighted…

I am capable of complete honesty
And that's a claim a lot of sons-o'-bitches
   freely make
All the friends I ever had are gone

An old man crossing two sets of train tracks
With a walker
In the ten-o'clock sun

An Ending

"I don't write about her anymore," I said
 So then … my writing days are over
"What colossally devastating misadventure might I
 adopt next?" I mused
"I'm not in a good way," I concluded
"Other than my mother, I don't give a hoot about
 making anyone on this earth proud of me,
 someday," I quipped
"It's like my soul is both ladle and soup," I surmised
"My will keeps dipping down but what's left is
 weaker than thin gruel," I postulated
"I offered up my innocence but got repaid with
 scorn," I quoted.
"So long … Fair thee well"
 She waved from the shore

"Lady Luck is just a charm"
"Get ahold of yourself, sailor!" spoke the captain

 I don't write about her any more
 My writing days are over

TIERS

My see-saw keeps a stiff upper lip
My tire-swing only dreams
My chaise-lounge has freckles
My hammock is clingy
My fan is always in a hurry
My fountain just babbles on … and on
My birdhouse feels used
My barbecue squints
My bar, I swear, has a mind of its own
My trampoline has had it
My rock garden ate too many butter-beans
My garden hose is *freaked*
My filter has indigestion
My cooler is sweating for some reason
My big umbrella switches feet
My parrots only gripe
How I hate them
My towels are asleep
My phone is a lobster from St. Pete.
My clothesline is out of tune
Only my windchime achieves nirvana
My bamboo stalks
My diving board is bored stiff
The slide thinks it's sexy

The dog…
I don't have a dog
The pool is filled with Scotch tape
My glass is full of paper clips…
I'm searching for my lost shaker of salt
The radio is *pumped…(clap)…up!*
My turtle has fallen and can't get up
There you go, Speedy

In the shrubs
Crickets and cicadas sing
A rare and different tune…

Look…
A rainbow!
How odd!

Acknowledgments

I would be remiss not to express my appreciation to my editor, Dave Bricker, sixth time around. If I'm spinning my wheels and don't know it, I can sense it from him. If I'm leaning too strong in one direction or another, he lets me know in so few words, it's painless. To properly thank him, I would have to have nine babbling, disheveled poets, all from different centuries, each deliver an entire oak tree of raw #2 pencils to his front door … in the rain … on a Tuesday.

Or maybe something a lot less nightmarish … say … to find an antique Vega guitar so hard and stiff and heavy that it cannot be damaged by conventional weapons (he only has nine guitars by his wife's last count).

Brick, you helped me get it together with a lot of class. And you keep strummin', man … 'cause someone has to.

—DW

www.ingramcontent.com/pod-product-compliance
Lightning Source LLC
Chambersburg PA
CBHW031139160426
43193CB00008B/190